MYTHS UNDERSTOOD

UNDERSTANDING INDIAN MYTHS

COLIN HYNSON

Crabtree Publishing Company
www.crabtreebooks.com

Author: Colin Hynson
Publishing plan research and development:
  Sean Charlebois, Reagan Miller
  Crabtree Publishing Company
Editor-in-chief: Lionel Bender
Editors: Simon Adams, Lynn Peppas
Proofreaders: Laura Booth, Wendy Scavuzzo
Project coordinator: Kathy Middleton
Photo research: Kim Richardson
Designer: Ben White
Cover design: Margaret Amy Salter
Production coordinator and Prepress technician:
  Margaret Amy Salter
Production: Kim Richardson
Print coordinator: Katherine Berti

Consultants: Amy Leggett-Caldera, M.Ed., Elementary
and Middle School Education Consultant, Mississippi
State University.

Cover: Meenakshi Temple (middle); Indian divinity
(bottom left and right); Indian deity (middle bottom)

Title page: Durga—the many-handed Indian deity

Photographs and reproductions:
Cover: Thinkstock (bottom), Shutterstock (middle)
Maps: Stefan Chabluk
Interior: The Art Archive: 5t (Palazzo Ducale Mantua/Superstock), 5b
(Musée du Louvre Paris/Collection Dagli Orti), 8–9 (Bibliothèque des
Arts Décoratifs Paris/Gianni Dagli Orti), 11 (Harper Collins
Publishers), 13 (Gianni Dagli Orti), 14 (Museo Capitolino
Rome/Gianni Dagli Orti), 16b (Musée du Louvre Paris/Collection
Dagli Orti), 18 (National Archaeological Museum Athens/Gianni Dagli
Orti), 19 (Archaeological Museum Florence/Gianni Dagli Orti), 22
(Bardo Museum Tunis/Gianni Dagli Orti), 38 (Museo Nazionale
Taranto/Gianni Dagli Orti). • Getty Images: (De Agostini): 24, 25, 26,
27, 30t, 29b, 33, 35, 36, 39; 29t (Photoservice Electa), 32 (Leemage), 44r
(Leemage). • The Kobal Collection: 43b (Warner Bros.). •
shutterstock.com: 1 (Nejron Photo), 4 (pandapaw), 6 (Kamira), 7
(S.Borisov), 9 (Peter Baxter), 10 (Shawn Hempel), 10–11 (Ivan Montero
Martinez), 16t (Paul Picone), 23 (Vadim Georgiev), 24 (Kamira), 30b
(Elnur), 31 (NesaCera), 34t (meirion Matthias), 34b (Olimpiu Pop), 40
(Dolgin Alexander Klimentyevich), 41 (c.), 42 (Volkov Roman), 42–43
(Antonio Abrignani), 43tl (Yuri Arcurs), 43tr (Andrey Burmakin), 44bl
(Junial Enterprises), 44br (Oleg Golovnev). • Topfoto (The Granger
Collection): 12–13, 20, 37, 40–41; (topfoto.co.uk): 15, 17 (Luisa
Ricciarini), 21 (World History Archive).

This book was produced for Crabtree Publishing Company
by Bender Richardson White

Library and Archives Canada Cataloguing in Publication

Hynson, Colin
        Understanding Indian myths / Colin Hynson.

(Myths understood)
Includes index.
Issued also in electronic formats.
ISBN 978-0-7787-4524-2 (bound).--ISBN 978-0-7787-4529-7 (pbk.)

        1. Mythology, Indic--Juvenile literature. 2. Hindu mythology
--Juvenile literature. 3. India--Religion--Juvenile literature. I. Title.
II. Series: Myths understood

BL2001.3.H96 2012   j294.5'13   C2012-906942-6

Library of Congress Cataloging-in-Publication Data

Hynson, Colin.
  Understanding Indian myths / Colin Hynson.
      pages cm. -- (Myths understood)
  Includes index.
  ISBN 978-0-7787-4524-2 (reinforced library binding) -- ISBN
978-0-7787-4529-7 (pbk.) -- ISBN 978-1-4271-9058-1 (electronic
(pdf) -- ISBN 978-1-4271-9112-0 (electronic (html)
  1. Mythology, Indic--Juvenile literature. 2. India--Religion--
Juvenile literature. 3. Hinduism--Juvenile literature. I. Title.

  BL2001.3.H96 2012
  294.5'13--dc23

                                                    2012041359

Crabtree Publishing Company

Printed in the U.S.A./112012/FA20121012

www.crabtreebooks.com   1-800-387-7650

Published in Canada
Crabtree Publishing
616 Welland Ave.
St. Catharines, Ontario
L2M 5V6

Published in the United States
Crabtree Publishing
PMB 59051
350 Fifth Avenue, 59th Floor
New York, New York 10118

Published in the United Kingdom
Crabtree Publishing
Maritime House
Basin Road North, Hove
BN41 1WR

Published in Australia
Crabtree Publishing
3 Charles Street
Coburg North
VIC 3058

CONTENTS

WHAT ARE MYTHS?

Myths are stories that were used in ancient times to explain the world in which people found themselves. Most were passed on by word of mouth, but some were written down. The myths told stories about the creation of the world, nature, family life, and about the Sun, Moon, and the seasons.

Ancient Indian myths not only explained the origins of the world, but also provided guides on how people should live their lives. This is especially important in India where, for thousands of years, people have believed in **reincarnation**—the continuous cycle of birth, life, death, and rebirth, and how it is influenced by good and bad behavior.

Unlike many other mythologies, the stories that came out of Ancient India still have an important role in India today. The beliefs of modern Hindus, Jains, and Buddhists emerged during the Mauryan and Gupta empires of Indian history, which lasted from approximately 500 B.C.E. to 500 C.E. In modern India, Buddhism has declined while Hinduism and Jainism remain the faiths of millions of people: Islam, Christianity, and Sikhism have all grown.

India has many sets of mythological stories. This is because of the vast size and varied geography and climate of India. Different religions, such as Hinduism, Buddhism, and Jainism, divided different parts of the region and also played a factor in the creation of multiple myths. All of the myths, however, have **Brahma** as the creator god and the most important figure.

SOURCES OF MYTHS

Many of the Ancient Indian myths can trace their origins to the Hindu epics known as the *Ramayana* and the *Mahabharata*. Both of these texts were written some time between 500 B.C.E. and 100 C.E. At more than 50,000 lines long, the *Ramayana* is the world's longest poem. It tells the story of Rama—who later became the Hindu preserver god **Vishnu**—and his wife Sita. The *Mahabharata* is a collection of stories such as the *Bhagavad Gita* and the *Rishyasringa*, which were written and then gathered together in the *Mahabharata* over several hundred years.

Below: This antique pottery tile shows the Hindu god Hanuman kneeling before the seated Lord Rama, his wife Sita, and her attendants.

Below: Hindu priests worship and give offerings to the great goddess Durga. In Hindu myths, Durga is a goddess capable of defeating demons and protecting gods and other goddesses.

LINK TO TODAY

Religion and myths have always been at the center of the way of life in India. The main religions in India are Hinduism, Buddhism, Islam, Sikhism, Christianity, and Jainism. Each of them has its own myths, houses of worship, festivals, holy sites, and religious art.

ANCIENT INDIA

The history of Ancient India is divided into three main periods. The first is known as the Vedic period. It lasted from about 1500 B.C.E. to 500 B.C.E. and saw the beginnings of the Hindu, Jain, and Buddhist faiths. The middle period saw the rise of the powerful Mauryan Empire that existed from about 321 B.C.E. to 185 B.C.E. The last part saw the rise of the Gupta Empire, which existed from 320 C.E. to 550 C.E.

The Vedic period is defined by a culture that arose in northern India. It is referred to as "Vedic" because it was at this time that the *Vedas*, the oldest Hindu **scriptures**, were first composed. In this period, the foundations of Hinduism were first laid. Little is known about everyday life in the Vedic period. People farmed in small communities and trade was done by exchanging goods. There was no money system so people did not buy and sell.

By about 1000 B.C.E., several small kingdoms or **city-states** known as the Mahajanapadas had begun to emerge. In about 500 B.C.E. there were 16 of these kingdoms stretching right across northern India. It was during this time that India saw the rise of cities such as Ayodhya, Panchala, and Rajpura. These new cities became the birthplace of both Jainism and Buddhism.

The Mauryan Empire was first established by King Chandragupta Maurya and reached its greatest extent in about 260 B.C.E. under Ashoka the Great. It extended across most of India and much of modern Pakistan and Afghanistan. Early in his reign, Ashoka was a cruel and violent king but he converted to Buddhism and became a more just and peaceful ruler. In 260 B.C.E., he made Buddhism the state religion. This helped to establish Buddhism in Ancient India although there was some opposition from his Hindu and Jain subjects.

India entered what is called the **golden age** when the Gupta Empire conquered much of the **subcontinent**. This empire, founded by Maharaja Sri Gupta, saw great advances in technology, astronomy, science, and the arts. The whole period saw the teachings of Hinduism, Buddhism, and Jainism develop. With the decline of the Gupta Empire, India broke up into smaller states and was not reunited until the Mughal Empire in the 1500s.

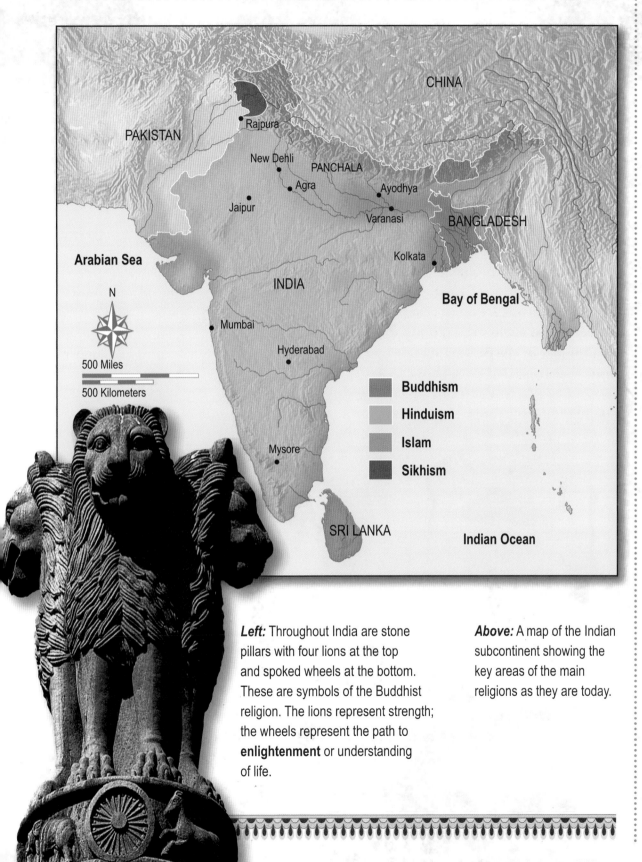

CHINA

PAKISTAN

Rajpura

New Dehli

PANCHALA

Agra

Ayodhya

Jaipur

Varanasi

BANGLADESH

Arabian Sea

Kolkata

N

INDIA

Bay of Bengal

Mumbai

500 Miles

Hyderabad

500 Kilometers

Buddhism

Hinduism

Islam

Mysore

Sikhism

SRI LANKA

Indian Ocean

Left: Throughout India are stone
pillars with four lions at the top
and spoked wheels at the bottom.
These are symbols of the Buddhist
religion. The lions represent strength;
the wheels represent the path to
enlightenment or understanding
of life.

Above: A map of the Indian
subcontinent showing the
key areas of the main
religions as they are today.

HINDU ROOTS AND BELIEFS

Almost all Indian myths are based on the spiritual traditions of Hinduism. These are a mix of duties related to family, each stage of life, and the society in which each person is born. Hindus believe that people who carry out these duties well will be rewarded with rebirth into a good life. Those that neglect their duties will be reborn into a life of poverty and suffering.

Although Hindus do not believe in one Supreme Being, all the gods and goddesses are linked together through the idea of **Brahman**, a **spirit** that exists in everything. All of the creation myths of Ancient India reflect these ideas and beliefs. Related myths refer to the preserver god Vishnu and the destroyer god **Shiva**, who plays a role in the creation and destruction of the Universe.

Below: An Indian illustration of the Universe from the 1600s. At the top, the god Vishnu rides on the giant bird, Garuda, which is linked to creation. Below, Vishnu sleeps on the serpent Ananta, which represents eternity. With him is the goddess **Lakshmi**.

CIRCULAR TIME

Hindu creation myths are different from many others because of the way that early Hindus viewed time. The creation of the Universe is not the beginning of time and its destruction is not the end. Hindus believe that the Universe is continually being created, destroyed, and made again. For Hindus, time is circular and has no start and no end.

BRAHMA CREATES THE UNIVERSE

The early beliefs and myths of Ancient Indian peoples were based around nature and gods who controlled natural forces. This creation myth, with **Brahma** as the creator of all things in the Universe, is typical.

Floating on the sea created by Lord Vishnu, the preserver of the Universe, was a giant golden egg. As the egg rocked on the gentle lapping waves of the sea, it began to grow and grow. Then a small crack appeared in the shell of the egg. The crack began to spread slowly from the top to the bottom of the egg, then around the other side of the egg. Eventually, the crack reached right around the egg and it split open.

   Brahma emerged from the egg. He took the two halves of the egg and from them the Universe was created. One half became the sky and inside that shell the Sun, other stars, the planets, and all the other heavenly bodies were made. The other half of the egg was turned into Earth. Inside this half, Brahma created all living things along with the oceans, mountains, and deserts.

Below: This illustration from about 1720 shows a woman giving a fire offering to please the Hindu divine triad, or group of three—Brahma, Vishnu, and Shiva (see page 10).

RELIGION *AND* GODS

The people of Ancient India worshiped many different gods and goddesses. The story of these deities **are told in the Hindu** epics **such as the *Ramayana* and the *Mahabharata* or myths passed on by storytellers through the generations.**

There was not one main god in Hinduism. The idea of Brahman first emerged in Vedic India. The Brahman was generally believed to be a type of spirit that seeps into everything within and outside of the Universe.

Hinduism in Ancient India had three main gods. Brahma was the creator of the Universe; Vishnu was the preserver and protector of the Universe; and Shiva destroyed the Universe so that it could be created again. Minor gods included Lakshmi, the goddess of

wealth and prosperity and the wife of Vishnu; Ushas, the goddess of the dawn; and Vayu, the god of the air and the wind. Many of these gods are related to one another either through birth or by marriage. Ancient Indians also believed in *maruts*. These were spirits of storms and thunder that rode through the sky in chariots.

Right: An illustration from he *Bala Kanda*—"Book of the Childhood"—from the *Ramayana*. It shows images of Brahma and other gods, a bear, and langur monkeys, helpers of the god Hanuman.

RAMA AND SITA

The story of Rama and Sita is one of the most important and best-known Ancient Indian myths. Rama and Sita are seen as having the ideal marriage that all couples should try to copy, for all time. Their story also gives the background and framework for the festival of Diwali.

Rama had been chosen by King Dasharatha to be the heir to the kingdom of Kosala. Rama was a very brave and wise man, and by his side was his beautiful and wise wife, Sita. However, Rama's stepmother plotted against him because she wanted her own son to become king. She convinced the king to banish Rama into the forest.

For many years, Rama and Sita lived a simple and contented life in the forest. One day, Rama and Sita saw a deer wandering among the trees. Sita thought it was the most beautiful creature she had ever seen and begged Rama to capture it to keep as a pet. Rama ran after the deer and left Sita alone.

All of a sudden, the demon Ravana swept down in his chariot and took Sita away to become his wife. As they flew through the air, Sita dropped her jewelry over the side of the chariot so that Rama could find her.

When Rama realized that Sita had been kidnapped, he followed the trail of gold and jewels left by Sita. The trail soon ran out but Rama had met the monkey Hanuman. With the help of an army of monkeys, Rama began the search for Sita. She was eventually found—as a prisoner on the island of Lanka.

Right: Dancers perform a ballet to celebrate Hanuman Jayanti, the birth of the god Hanuman. Often represented by a monkey, the god is a symbol of strength and energy, and has magical powers and the ability to conquer evil spirits.

WORSHIP AND PRAYER

In Ancient India, worship of the gods mostly took place in the home. It took the form of offering food and drink to the gods as a gift known as *puja*. The rituals were called *upacharas* and were centered around a shrine built in the house. A shrine was usually dedicated to just one god.

Worship in Hindu temples was not seen as something that had to be done. Visits to the temple were reserved for festivals or for special occasions such as a wedding. Each temple worshiped one set of gods, so it was important to visit the correct temple.

Bhakti was an important part of Hindu ritual. This was the idea that people had to show a personal and active **devotion** to one particular god. This could take the form of chanting the name of the god over and over or by the way a person lived his or her everyday life.

Below: A woman holds Diwali festival candles, which are lit and placed in windows to attract the attention of the goddess Lakshmi.

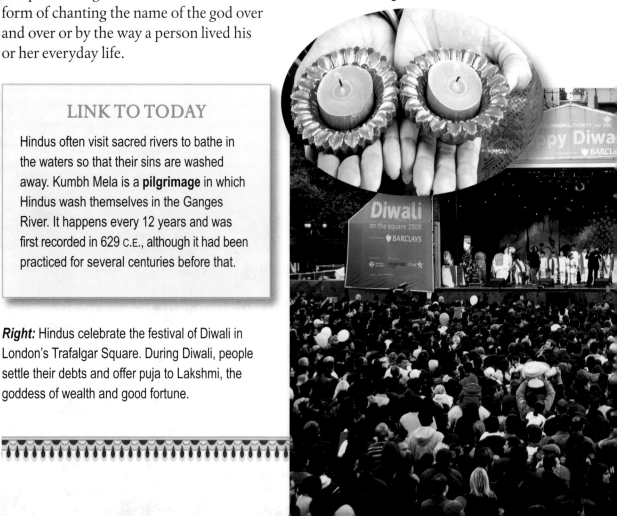

LINK TO TODAY

Hindus often visit sacred rivers to bathe in the waters so that their sins are washed away. Kumbh Mela is a **pilgrimage** in which Hindus wash themselves in the Ganges River. It happens every 12 years and was first recorded in 629 C.E., although it had been practiced for several centuries before that.

Right: Hindus celebrate the festival of Diwali in London's Trafalgar Square. During Diwali, people settle their debts and offer puja to Lakshmi, the goddess of wealth and good fortune.

Above: During a puja ceremony, a Hindu priest anoints a worshiper with an offering to the goddess Durga.

ARJUNA AND THE HUNTER

The story of Arjuna is told in the epic *Mahabharata*. Arjuna was a prince who could only defeat his enemies with the aid of a magical weapon. He had to show a personal devotion to Shiva before he could be given the weapon.

Arjuna knew that if he was to be given the magical weapon he had to show penance, or regret for wrongdoings. He traveled through the forest until he reached the mountain called Indrakila. There he met an old man who taunted him, telling him that he would never show enough penance to earn the approval of Shiva. Arjuna ignored his harsh words and replied that his only aim was to please Shiva. At that point, the old man revealed himself as Arjuna's father in disguise and gave him his blessing.

Arjuna's penance continued. In the first month, he ate only every three days, then every six days in the second month, and so on until by the fifth month he was living only on air. He also stood on just one leg for several days as he concentrated all of his thoughts on Shiva.

Shortly afterward, Shiva went into the forest to go hunting. Both Shiva and Arjuna saw a demon disguised as a boar. They both carefully put an arrow on their bows and both took aim. They fired and the arrows hit the boar and it was killed.

Shiva and Arjuna argued about which arrow had killed the boar. Arjuna lost his temper and showered a rain of arrows on Shiva who caught them all in flight. Shiva and Arjuna then began to wrestle. Arjuna was thrown to the ground. On the ground, Arjuna closed his eyes and prayed to Shiva to help him. When he opened his eyes, he saw that the hunter was Shiva. He blessed Arjuna's strength and devotion and gave him the magical weapon.

THE PARADE OF THE ANTS

This story is told to show the central importance of karma **in the idea of reincarnation. Hindus believe that, in the revolving cycle of life and death, what we are reborn as depends on our previous lives.**

The king of the gods, Indra, was proud of his victory over the demon Vritra. He called on Vishvakarman to build him a palace fit for a king who destroyed all his enemies. Every time Vishvakarman showed him a new design for the palace, Indra rejected it as not being grand enough.

In the end, Vishvakarman complained to Brahma about Indra's pride. Brahma sent Vishnu to Indra disguised as a young boy. Vishnu met with Indra and asked him when the palace would be finished as he had seen many palaces built by other proud Indras in the past. The boy then saw a huge procession of ants passing through the palace. He explained that every ant had once been king of the gods but had fallen in status because of its karma. Indra saw what pride would do and ordered an end to the building of the palace.

Right: The Hindu elephant-headed god **Ganesh** sits before the wheel of life and death. Ganesh is the god of good luck and wisdom. For Buddhists, the eight-spoked wheel represents the path to enlightenment.

CYCLES OF LIFE AND DEATH

One of the central beliefs of all Hindus in Ancient India was a belief in reincarnation. The belief is that everyone goes through a continuous cycle of birth, death, and rebirth. When someone dies, their spirit moves on to another living thing, which does not have to be a human—it can be any animal. This continuous process was known as *samsara*. Reincarnation was first mentioned in Vedic writings between 1700 B.C.E. and 1100 B.C.E.

The way that a person lived their lives determined how they would be born again after they had died. This was decided by each person's karma. This is an ancient Indian word that means "action." Karma describes the belief that every action that someone does will create a reaction in the future. A good deed will result in a good reaction, but a sin, crime, or act of hatred creates a bad reaction. If someone has good karma when they die, then their rebirth will be joyful, happy, and rewarding.

POWER TO DO GOOD

Along with karma, Ancient Indians were also concerned with *dharma.* Dharma was the power that maintained order in the world and gave people the ability to behave well. Each person had his or her *sva-dharma* that allowed them to act **virtuously**. Each person had different ways of behaving correctly and it was up to them to find out what they were.

Below: Mourners gather at Manikarnika Ghat on the banks of the Ganges River, the most important place for Hindus to be cremated. Bodies are cremated to allow the soul to journey to its next destination.

BUDDHISM AND JAINISM

The two other faiths of Ancient India that arose toward the end of the Vedic period were Buddhism and Jainism. Both of these faiths shared many beliefs with Hindus but there are also some important differences that are reflected in their myths, traditions, customs, and ceremonies.

The history of Buddhism begins with the life of one man, Siddhartha Gautama, known as Buddha. His birth and death dates are not known for sure, but are believed to be between 490 and 410 B.C.E. After an early life of luxury, he left home to live a life of self-denial as he tried to find a way to exist without any suffering. Eventually he found **enlightenment**—an awareness of one's path in life—and became the Buddha. He then spent the rest of his life spreading his teachings.

THE DREAMS OF MOTHER TRISHALA

This story is one of the best-known of the Jain myths. It is a prophecy **of the birth of Mahavira, who is seen as the founder of the Jain faith. Mahavira was the last of the Tirthankaras, who the Jains believe are great teachers.**

Queen Trishala was expecting a baby. She found her husband King Siddhartha to share the good news with him. He was overjoyed that he was going to become a father and ordered celebrations throughout their land.

After the excitement of the day, Siddhartha slept a dreamless and undisturbed night. Trishala, on the other hand, kept on waking up. She had 14 bright and vivid dreams, and she knew that they were signs about the child that she was carrying.

In the morning, she called together all of the wise men in the kingdom and asked them what her dreams meant. The first three dreams were of a white elephant, a bull, and a lion. The wise men told her that this meant that her son would have a good character, be very spiritual, and would be fearless. Her other dreams all showed that her son was destined to be a great religious leader. The last dream was of a huge fire without smoke. The wise men said that fire cleans away old ideas and beliefs, and leaves the ground ready for new truths to take root. Mahavira was that flame.

It is more difficult to trace the beginnings of Jainism. Jains believed that their faith was as old as the Universe, but that its teachings have slowly been revealed by people called *Tirthankaras*. The first Tirthankara was Adinatha, who was alive at the beginning of time. The last Tirthankara was Mahavira. He was born around 600 B.C.E. Like Siddhartha, Mahavira was born into a royal family but gave this up to live a simple life. His teachings began to spread through India around 300 B.C.E.

The Buddhists and Jains shared one belief with Hindus—they believed in reincarnation and in the concepts of karma and dharma. However, neither the Buddhist nor the Jain faith had any gods or goddesses to worship. These traditions have continued to the present-day.

CHANGING FAITHS

Buddhism began to decline in India after the fall of the Gupta Empire, when Indian rulers began to show greater support for Hinduism. Many Buddhist temples were converted into Hindu places of worship. Buddhism almost disappeared from India after the Muslim conquest of India that started in 712 C.E.

Right: A Jain painting of a Jina, also known as a Tirthankara. Central to Jain beliefs and myths is nonviolence. Jains try to avoid violence toward any living thing—people, animals, and plants.

THE NATURAL WORLD

In Ancient India, there were two great rivers that played an important part in the lives of many people. They were the Indus and the Ganges. Both played a central part in the development of Hinduism and its myths, and in the working lives of ordinary people.

Below: To this day, Hindus wash themselves in the Ganges to purify their bodies and minds.

WASHED CLEAN OF SINS

Every year in spring, Hindus in Ancient India traveled to the Ganges to celebrate Ganga Dashahara—the descent of the river from Heaven to Earth. Washing in the Ganges during this time was believed to cleanse the bather of ten lifetimes of sin.

THE CREATION OF THE GANGES

The story of the creation of the Ganges River is a complicated one that involves the ashes of the many sons of King Sagara, his grandson King Bhagiratha, and the god Indra who was jealous of Sagara. The story also explains why the Ganges is seen as a place of purification.

King Bhagiratha knew that the only way the remains of the 60,000 sons of his grandfather were to be saved would be by washing them in heavenly water. He called on Brahma to bring the waters of the goddess Ganga to Earth. Brahma promised that he would do this. But Earth would not withstand the impact of Ganga crashing down from heaven, so Shiva was chosen to lower her down gently.

After a year, Shiva agreed to carry Ganga on his head. The water crashed down and hit him. Unfortunately, Ganga became lost in his hair and spent many years trying to find a way out before the water trickled down his body and flowed onto the ground. When the water touched Shiva's body, it became pure and could wash away all sins. King Bhagiratha led the way in his royal chariot and the water followed. When the water reached the ocean, it entered a huge hole in which the ashes of the 60,000 sons lay. The moment the ashes came into contact with the water, the sons ascended into the world of the gods.

The Indus River starts in modern-day Tibet and travels through northern India before coming out at the Arabian Sea in what is now the coast of Pakistan. The river is just under 2,000 miles (3,219 km) long. The lands around the Indus were especially fertile, or rich in nutrients, and it gave rise to the first great civilization in India. The Indus Valley Civilization existed between 3300 B.C.E. and 1300 B.C.E. and it centered on such great cities as Harrapa, Lothal, and Kalibanga.

The Ganges begins in the Himalaya Mountains in northern India and flows more than 1,500 miles (2,414 km) to the Bay of Bengal in modern-day Bangladesh. The decline of the Indus Valley Civilization saw the rise of the Ganges as an important place to settle during the Vedic period of Ancient India.

Of the two rivers, the Ganges took on a more important role in Hindu myths and in religious practices. The Ganges was a sacred river. Its waters were seen as pure and having the power to wash away sins. The cremated remains of the dead were also thrown into the Ganges to help with reincarnation.

In India, the monsoon season—weeks of heavy rain—is between June and September. It is the most important part of the farming year. In Vedic myths, it was believed that the monsoon came after a battle between Indra the Lord of Heaven and Vritra, a dragon that blocked rivers causing droughts.

Left: A street scene in Varanasi during a monsoon.

HARVESTS AND AGRICULTURE

In Ancient India, as now, agriculture depended on fertile soil and a ready supply of water to feed the crops. Therefore, farming was concentrated around the great rivers of the Ganges and the Indus, as well as others such as the Kaveri and Godavari.

There is evidence that crops have been grown in Ancient India since 9000 B.C.E. It was only much later, in the Indus Valley Civilization, that irrigation was first used to feed crops and to take water to other farming areas. In about 220 C.E., the Grand Anicut Dam was built across the Kaveri to supply water to local farmers.

During the Vedic period, from 1500 B.C.E. to 500 B.C.E., the main crops grown were wheat and barley. Those two crops did not need as much water as other crops. With the rise of the Mauryan Empire a few hundred years later, irrigation through the use of dams and canals became more common. That meant different crops, such as rice and millet, could be grown.

Right: During the festival of Holi, which marks the arrival of spring, people throw brightly colored paint powders at each other. The festival is high-spirited, with bonfires, music, practical jokes, good fun, and dancing in the streets.

PRAHLAD AND HOLIKA

The spring festival of Holi is one of the most important in the Hindu calendar. It celebrates the start of a new season and the promise of a good harvest. It is also a very colorful festival that reflects the abundant colors of spring. The story of Prince Prahlad and the witch Holika is remembered during Holi.

King Hiranyakashipu was an evil demon king who had conquered all of Heaven and had turned the gods into his servants. Hiranyakashipu had overthrown Indra, the Lord of Heaven, and made himself king of the gods.

Hiranyakashipu had a son named Prahlad. One day after he had returned from his lessons, Prahlad's father asked him what he had learned. Prahlad said that it was that Vishnu was the highest among the gods.

Hiranyakashipu flew into a rage at his son's answer and tried to change his mind, but it was impossible. His son remained devoted to Vishnu. Eventually his father decided to have him killed. He had Prahlad thrown into a pit of snakes, where he was fed poisonous food and was trampled upon by a herd of elephants. Every time, Prahlad was protected by Vishnu.

The king turned to his sister, a witch named Holika, to finally kill his son. She built a huge bonfire, then called to Prahlad to join her. She promised that they could walk through the fire together and not be harmed. They walked into the flames. Vishnu pulled Prahlad from the fire and left Holika to perish.

PLANTS AND ANIMALS

Plants and animals were key to the religious and everyday lives of the people of Ancient India. As a result, they appear in many of the myths that were developed at that time.

The lotus flower became an important symbol for purity and beauty in Vedic India. Later on, images appeared of Vishnu and Lakshmi standing on a lotus flower. Buddhists believed that lotus flowers bloomed everywhere that the Buddha walked, and he is often portrayed sitting on a lotus flower.

Cows were important in Ancient Indian society. During the Vedic period, cattle were seen as a source of wealth and were often given as gifts. By the time of the Gupta Empire, 300 C.E. to 550 C.E., killing a cow became punishable by death. Cows had become sacred animals that could not be harmed.

There are several gods and goddesses that had an animal form. The best-known are Ganesh, the god of wisdom; and Prithvi, the goddess of Earth. Ganesh has the head of an elephant and Prithvi has the head of a cow.

Right: A figure of Ganesh is paraded through the streets of Hyderabad during a Hindu festival.

CAUSE NO HARM

Jains and Buddhists believed that all living things should be well cared for and no unnecessary harm should come to any animal or plant. Most Jains and Buddhists are vegetarian.

LINK TO TODAY

Cows are still seen as sacred in modern India. It is illegal to kill a cow in India and Hindus will not eat beef. Their treatment of cattle gave rise to the phrase "sacred cow."

Right: Sacred cows walk along a street in Dehli. People and traffic get out of their way. Cattle are considered sacred by Hindus, as they were by many people in parts of Ancient Egypt, Greece, and Rome.

THE CREATION OF GANESH

Ganesh remains one of the most popular of the Hindu gods. He is seen as the bringer of good luck. Whenever something new is started, Hindus often turn to Ganesh to bring them good fortune. There is more than one story about the creation of Ganesh. The main story comes from the *Shiva Purana,* a religious text related to Shiva.

Parvati wanted to take a bath, but there was nobody to guard the door to make sure she was not interrupted. She made the figure of a boy out of turmeric paste, gave him life, named him Ganesh, and ordered him not to allow anyone into the house.

After a while, Parvati's husband Shiva returned home and tried to get past Ganesh. Ganesh blocked his path and refused to let him past. Shiva was not used to being challenged. Shiva had a fierce battle with Ganesh in which Ganesh's head was severed.

When Parvati saw what had happened, she demanded that Shiva restore life to Ganesh at once. Shiva promised to do so and went in search of the missing head. He could not find Ganesh's original head, so Shiva cut the head off of an elephant and stuck it on Ganesh's body before bringing him back to life.

DAILY LIFE

Hindus in Ancient India believed that the Universe was created out of chaos and it was important that this disorder and destruction were kept at bay.

One way of doing this was by creating an ordered society in which people knew what their duties and obligations would be. The gods of Ancient India, especially Brahma, were also involved in making sure that order was maintained.

The **caste** system in Ancient India was a way of making sure that order could function on Earth. At birth, people were placed into one of four main castes, or *varnas*. Marriage was only allowed among people of the same caste. With marriage, varnas became subdivided into smaller groups called *jatis*.

The varnas were Brahmins, Kshatriyas, Vaishyas, and Shudras. The Brahmins were priests who dedicated their lives to living a pure life. The Kshatriyas were warriors and soldiers. The Vaishyas involve themselves in trade and farming. The Shudras were servants. There were also some people who were not members of any of the varnas. They were known as Chandalas or Dalits, meaning **outcasts**, untouchables, or the downtrodden.

Below: At a Hindu cremation, a member of the untouchable caste leads the ceremony. Women are not permitted.

BY NATURE OR ACTIONS?

The origins of the caste system can be found in writings such as the *Bhagavad Gita* from the Vedic period. Later Hindu writing, such as the *Ramayana* and the *Mahabharata,* also mention the caste system but say that caste is decided by behavior not birth.

THE STORY OF PURUSHA

The *Rigveda* is an ancient text that was composed in the early Vedic period of Ancient India. It contains several hymns praising the gods, and mythical stories about the creation of the Universe. One of these stories is of Purusha, which relates the tale of how the four castes were created.

When the gods wanted to make the Universe and all of the things that were in it, they looked around for something to build the Universe with. Purusha was a huge and terrible giant with 1,000 feet and 1,000 heads. The gods talked among themselves and decided that Purusha would be sacrificed and his body cut up to make the world.

In the moment that he died, the first Hindu hymns were created and animals began to be born. The Moon was made from his mind. The stars and the heavens were made from his skull, and the Sun came from his eyes. Indra, the king of the gods, emerged from his mouth.

Other parts of his body were used to create all of the people of the world. The Brahmins came from his mouth, the Kshatriyas emerged from his arms, the Vaishyas were made from his arms, and the Shudras from his many feet.

25

Above: The Buddhist temple of Mahabodhi was built by the Emperor Ashoka. It is believed to be the place where Buddha was enlightened.

CITY-STATES

The Gupta Empire lasted from 320 C.E. to 550 C.E. and stretched across much of what is modern India. During this period, great strides were made in science, technology, engineering, architecture, literature, and mathematics.

This "golden age" of Indian history came about because the Gupta Empire created order and stability throughout all of the land, and set up trade links with **Arabia**, China, and Southeast Asia. Many of the kings were also interested in extending learning among their subjects. King Chandragupta II, who reigned from 380 to 415, encouraged many artists and scholars. Although he was a Hindu, he also supported Buddhist and Jain cultures.

During the Gupta Empire, it is believed that literacy and numeracy increased. Teachers traveled around the country, educating common people and also passing on myths and their own beliefs. It was also a time when several universities were created, making India a center of learning. The two main universities were Nalanda and Takshashila.

A STELLAR HINDU

Varahamihira was an astronomer and mathematician who worked at the court of King Chandragupta. His study of the stars and planets laid the foundations for other astronomers to discover the orbits of the planets, as well as estimate their diameters.

LINK TO TODAY

The number system that we use today—the symbols for one to nine—was first developed in India during the Gupta Empire. Known as the Hindu-Arabic Numeral System, it was used in Europe after 1200 C.E. and replaced the number system used by the Romans.

THE STORY OF SARASWATI

Saraswati is one of the most admired of the Hindu goddesses. She is the goddess of knowledge, music, the arts, and the sciences. As learning became more important in India, the number of myths about Saraswati increased. Saraswati has often been depicted with four arms and sitting on a lotus flower.

When Brahma created the Universe, he saw that there was chaos everywhere. He looked around and yearned for some order to be brought to the world that he had made, but he did not know how to do this. Then he heard a voice that told him that only knowledge would turn chaos into order. So from his mouth came Saraswati. She was clothed in white and rode on a swan. In one hand, she held a book. In the other hand, she held a musical instrument.

Brahma asked Saraswati how she could help him create order in this new world he had created. She began to play her musical instrument. The soothing music began to replace the roar of confusion that was all around them. Chaos turned into the stars, the Sun, and the Moon. The oceans filled with water and the seasons started to change. From then on Brahma always kept Saraswati by his side as a source of wisdom.

Right: A statuette of the goddess Saraswati.

THE STRUCTURE OF SOCIETY

At the top of Indian society was a king or emperor. Below that was the caste system. At first, the caste system was rigid. A person's caste, and the tasks they would do as adults, were decided at birth. By the arrival of the Gupta Empire, the caste system had become more flexible but was still important.

It was rare for women in Ancient India to hold any position of power, and many of them spent their adult lives working with their husbands and caring for their home and children. However, in the Vedic period, the education of girls was encouraged and several female scholars were mentioned in Vedic literature. During the Gupta Empire, the education of women had become less important and they also lost the right to hold their own property after marriage.

Clothing in Ancient India was mostly made from cotton. Women wore one long piece of cloth that was called a *sari*. This could be wrapped around the body in many different ways. Men also wore a piece of cloth called a *dhoti* that covered the legs, and a simple shirt.

THE STORY OF DRAUPADI

Draupadi appears in the *Mahabharata* and is one of the most admired women in Hinduism. Although she is not a goddess, she is close to Krishna. She tends to Krishna when he cuts his finger, then is protected by him. She is most famous for having five husbands at the same time.

The Pandava prince Arjuna had defeated King Drupada in battle and took away half of his kingdom. Drupada knew he could never win his kingdom back through the battlefield. So he performed a fire sacrifice from which his daughter, the beautiful Draupadi, emerged.

Drupada wanted Prince Arjuna to marry Draupadi. All the other four Pandava princes wanted to marry her so Drupada set them a challenge. They had to hit a revolving target with an arrow that they could only see in the reflection of a silver bowl. Drupada believed that only Arjuna had the skill to win the challenge. He was right. Arjuna hit the target and claimed Draupadi as his wife.

When Arjuna and his brothers returned home, they told their mother Kunti that Arjuna brought back a great prize with him. Kunti had always told them that they had to share everything they had equally among themselves. Before she had the chance to hear about Draupadi, she ordered Arjuna to share his prize. Arjuna obeyed his mother and all five brothers took Draupadi as their wife.

Left: This historic illustration from the *Bhagavad Gita* shows the battle scene between Arjuna (far right), helped by Krishna (in front of him) and his soldiers (at the bottom) and King Drupada (on the elephant) and his forces (on the left).

GURUS

Hindus believe that people pass through four stages of life (see page 30). A person in the final stage may become a *guru*, or spiritual teacher, teaching a good life by example. Gurus give up all links with the modern material society in which they live in preparation for leaving this world at the time of death.

RITUALS OF LIFE

In early Hinduism, a series of rituals called the *samskaras* were developed to mark important stages in a person's life. These began before a baby was even born. There were special rituals at the third and seventh months of pregnancy. After birth, the baby was welcomed into the world with a

Below: A traditional Hindu wedding in Chennai, Tamil Nadu, India. A prospective wife's parents choose a husband with her permission then use an astrological calendar to select the wedding day.

ceremony called *Jatakarma*. There were several more rituals and ceremonies for babies and children, such as the first hair cut and the first day at school.

The rituals continued at key stages in a person's life. The two most important were when a person got married and when he or she died. The wedding ceremony was called *Vivah Sanskar*. Once a person died, they went through a ritual known as *Antyesti*. The process differed according to caste, but it involved the body being washed and cremated.

GETTING MARRIED

There were many stages in the marriage ritual. In the first stage, the bride's parents welcomed the groom's family into their home. The wedding carried on until the most important part—the ceremony of vows. In the last stage, the bride left her home and went to live in the groom's parents' home.

LINK TO TODAY

All of the ancient ceremonies are maintained by modern Hindus. However, Hindus living in Europe and North America have had to change the rituals for cremation of deceased relatives. In Europe and North America, it is illegal to carry out a cremation in the open air.

THE BIRTH OF KRISHNA

Every year, Hindus celebrate the birthday of Krishna in a joyous festival called Janmashtami. A cloth-covered cradle is placed on an altar and when midnight comes—the time when Krishna was born—the cloth is removed to reveal a picture of the baby Krishna inside. This myth tells the story.

The kingdom of Mathura was ruled by a cruel king named Kamsa. He had a sister named Devaki, who was as good as Kamsa was bad. She lived quietly in the king's palace with her husband, Vasudeva.

One day, all three were out walking when a voice was heard telling Kamsa he would be killed by the eighth child of his sister. Kamsa flew into a rage and ordered that Devaki and Vasudeva be thrown into prison. There they remained for many years. They had seven children and each one was killed by Kamsa within minutes of being born.

Krishna saw what was happening. He decided that he would protect Devaki and Vasudeva by being born as the eighth child himself. His birth was a time of great joy and also of great fear. The gods helped Vasudeva carry Krishna out of the prison. He then switched Krishna for the baby daughter of a cowherd and returned to the prison.

The next morning, Kamsa ordered that the baby girl be killed. However, the girl flew in to the sky and returned home. Kamsa sent his soldiers out to kill every baby boy they could find, but Krishna was never found.

Below: Hindus wash themselves in the sea before entering the temple at the celebration of Ram Navami, the birth of Lord Rama.

HOLY DAYS

As the beliefs of Hinduism developed during the Vedic and Mauryan Empire periods, several days in the Hindu calendar became festivals or holy days. On these important occasions, people gathered together to worship. Many of the festivals involved joyous and colorful celebrations.

The holy days were usually linked to a particular god or goddess about whom there were many myths. Ganesh Chaturthi was a special day to celebrate the birthday of Ganesh. Shiva had a special festival dedicated to him, which was called Mahashivratri. Worshipers fasted during the festival but offered food to Shiva. During Rama Navami, which celebrated the birth of Rama, houses were cleaned before offerings were placed on the family shrine. In temples, the story of Rama is told continuously during the festivities in readings from the *Ramayana*.

THE DEVOTION OF LUBDHAKA

Mahashivratri is a festival dedicated to the god Shiva. Many of the celebrations take place when the Sun has gone down because Shiva is often associated with darkness. The myth of Lubdhaka is often told during the festival because it takes place at night.

One night, a poor man and a worshiper of Shiva named Lubdhaka went into the deep forest to collect some firewood. It had been raining so it was difficult to find any dry wood. Lubdhaka went much farther into the forest than he had planned, and he soon found that he was lost. Not only did he not recognize the trees around him, but the light was beginning to fade and the cloak of darkness began to spread across the forest canopy.

In the darkness, Lubdhaka climbed a tree and waited for dawn to arrive. The silence of the forest was broken by the cries and growls of tigers and other wild animals. Some of them passed right under the tree where Lubdhaka was hiding, but not one looked up.

Lubdhaka knew that he had to keep himself alert and awake until daybreak. He plucked one leaf at a time from the tree and dropped it to the ground, while chanting the name of Shiva.

By the time the Sun had risen, Lubdhaka had dropped thousands of leaves onto the ground. Shiva was pleased by Lubdhaka's all-night worship and made sure that he was never harmed by a wild animal.

Two of the greatest Hindu festivals were Navarati and Diwali. Navarati, or Nine Nights, was a festival that took place over nine days and celebrated the mother goddess Durga. It also marked a celebration of the ending of the harvest. Diwali was a festival of light, with lamps being burned and fireworks being set off. It marked the triumph of good over evil and of light over darkness. It was a time for gift-giving between families. Diwali was also celebrated by Jains.

LINK TO TODAY

Many of the holy days are still celebrated by modern Hindus around the world. In 2009, President Obama was the first American president to celebrate Diwali in the White House in Washington D.C. with members of America's Hindu community.

Below: Hindus dance in the street as they celebrate the birth of Ganesh, mythical god of new endeavors, in the Flushing neighborhood of New York City.

TRADE *AND* WARFARE

The earliest evidence of trade goods being exchanged between India and the Middle East dates back to Vedic times. Ancient Indian objects have been found in the Middle East in places such as modern-day Oman, Iran, and Iraq.

It was during the Mauryan Empire, 321 B.C.E. to 180 B.C.E., that trade with the outside world began to grow quickly. Trade with the Ancient Greeks started in about 300 B.C.E., but the most important trading partners at this time were the Ancient Romans. Roman pottery, coins, tools, and other objects have been found in western India. Goods were transported by ships, with Roman vessels traveling across the Red Sea and up the Arabian Gulf to the Mediterranean.

The main trade items that Ancient India had to offer were spices and incense, which could not be grown in Europe. The spices were important to provide flavoring for food. They were very expensive and only the wealthiest Romans could afford to buy them. Animals such as monkeys, elephants, and tigers were also sent to Rome from India, mostly as curiosities.

Trade in other goods, especially **textiles** made from cotton and silk, also grew during the Mauryan Empire. Ancient Indian textiles have also been found in Ancient Rome, Egypt, Madagascar, and in ports along the East African coast.

THE CHURNING OF THE MILKY OCEANS

Lakshmi is the goddess of wealth, trade, and prosperity. This myth is meant to show that Lakshmi will bless anyone with success and good fortune as long as he or she works hard. Greed and the love of money will take these blessings away, however.

Indra, the king of the gods, had been given the task of protecting the world from demons. For many years, with the blessing of Lakshmi, he had successfully kept the demons at bay. A wise man gave Indra a garland of sacred flowers as a gift. Indra threw them on to the floor, because he believed that he should be given a much greater gift.

Upset by Indra's display of arrogance, Lakshmi left the world of the gods and entered the milky ocean. Without her, the gods were no longer blessed with good fortune. People became greedy and no longer made offerings in their temples. Demons began to take control of the world.

Indra turned to Vishnu for advice. Vishnu told him that the gods would have to churn the milky ocean until Lakshmi would emerge. The gods churned the oceans for more than 1,000 years, until a woman standing on a lotus flower rose from the water. It was Lakshmi, who had returned to the world. With her help, the gods eventually defeated the demons and chased them out of the world.

Right: A brightly colored carving of the Hindu goddess Lakshmi.

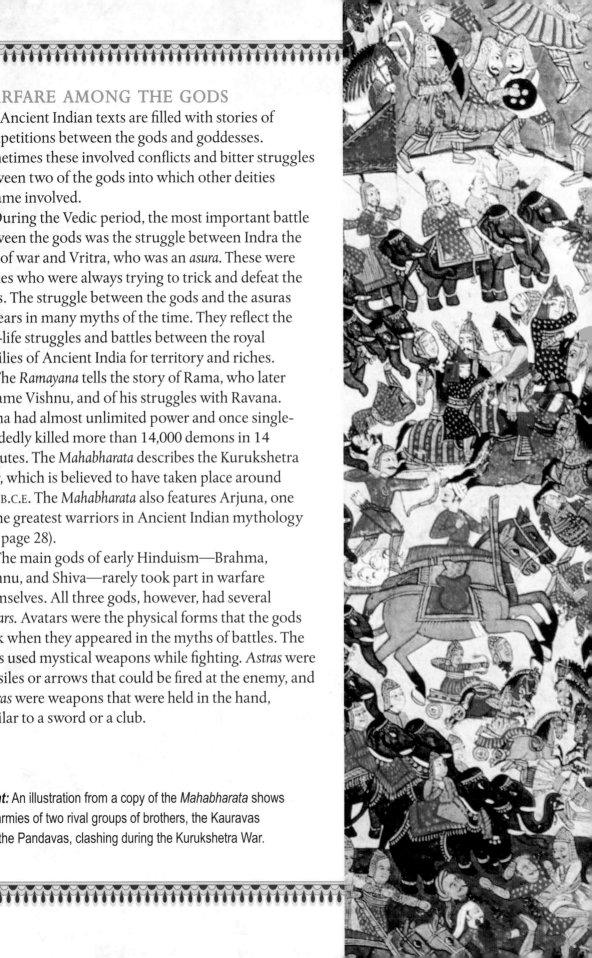

WARFARE AMONG THE GODS

The Ancient Indian texts are filled with stories of competitions between the gods and goddesses. Sometimes these involved conflicts and bitter struggles between two of the gods into which other deities became involved.

During the Vedic period, the most important battle between the gods was the struggle between Indra the god of war and Vritra, who was an *asura*. These were deities who were always trying to trick and defeat the gods. The struggle between the gods and the asuras appears in many myths of the time. They reflect the real-life struggles and battles between the royal families of Ancient India for territory and riches.

The *Ramayana* tells the story of Rama, who later became Vishnu, and of his struggles with Ravana. Rama had almost unlimited power and once single-handedly killed more than 14,000 demons in 14 minutes. The *Mahabharata* describes the Kurukshetra War, which is believed to have taken place around 900 B.C.E. The *Mahabharata* also features Arjuna, one of the greatest warriors in Ancient Indian mythology (see page 28).

The main gods of early Hinduism—Brahma, Vishnu, and Shiva—rarely took part in warfare themselves. All three gods, however, had several *avatars.* Avatars were the physical forms that the gods took when they appeared in the myths of battles. The gods used mystical weapons while fighting. *Astras* were missiles or arrows that could be fired at the enemy, and *sastras* were weapons that were held in the hand, similar to a sword or a club.

Right: An illustration from a copy of the *Mahabharata* shows the armies of two rival groups of brothers, the Kauravas and the Pandavas, clashing during the Kurukshetra War.

THE THREE CITIES IN THE SKY

This story of Shiva destroying three anti-god cities that floated in the sky with a single arrow shows that the gods sometimes tried to deceive one another to gain supremacy.

The asura, or anti-god, Taraka had three sons. After Taraka's death, his sons decided to follow lives of devotion. They retreated into the forest and meditated for more than 1,000 years. Brahma told them they could have anything they desired. They asked for **immortality** but Brahma could not give it to them. Taraka's sons then asked for three cities, each stocked with riches and strongly **fortified**. All three cities were to be **mobile** so that they could move across the sky.

After the cities were built, Indra and some of the other gods grew suspicious of the three **pious** men. Shiva refused to do anything about them because they were his **devotees**. The gods then approached Vishnu who agreed to help them.

Vishnu created a wise man who went into the cities and convinced the three men to stop their worship of Shiva. The people in the three cities also began to behave badly and they neglected their devotions to the gods. The gods then approached Shiva again. He agreed that the three cities had strayed from the path of virtue and had to be destroyed. Shiva waited for thousands of years until the three moving cities were joined together. He then fired a burning arrow. The arrow set all three cities alight and they were reduced to ashes.

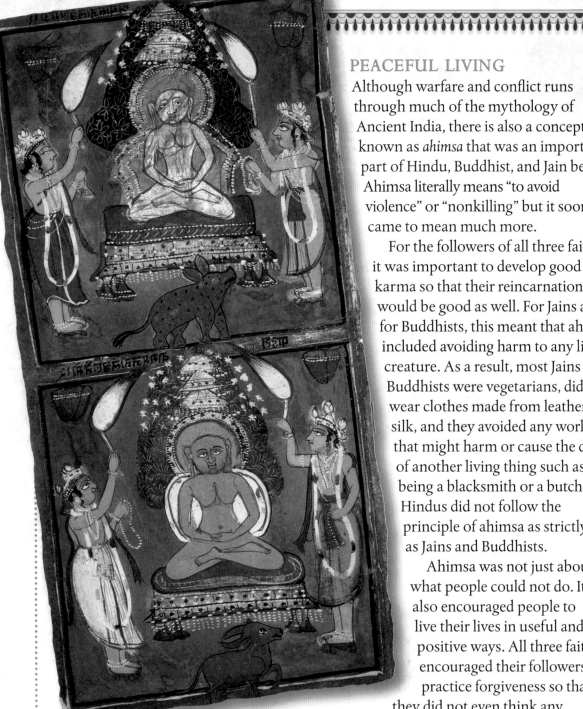

PEACEFUL LIVING

Although warfare and conflict runs through much of the mythology of Ancient India, there is also a concept known as *ahimsa* that was an important part of Hindu, Buddhist, and Jain beliefs. Ahimsa literally means "to avoid violence" or "nonkilling" but it soon came to mean much more.

For the followers of all three faiths, it was important to develop good karma so that their reincarnation would be good as well. For Jains and for Buddhists, this meant that ahimsa included avoiding harm to any living creature. As a result, most Jains and Buddhists were vegetarians, did not wear clothes made from leather or silk, and they avoided any work that might harm or cause the death of another living thing such as being a blacksmith or a butcher. Hindus did not follow the principle of ahimsa as strictly as Jains and Buddhists.

Ahimsa was not just about what people could not do. It also encouraged people to live their lives in useful and positive ways. All three faiths encouraged their followers to practice forgiveness so that they did not even think any harmful thoughts. The Mauryan emperor Ashoka the Great was a devoted follower of ahimsa. He abolished slavery, reformed his prisons, and banned hunting and fishing throughout his empire.

Above: An Indian painting from 1720 of two of the 24 Tirthankaras, or teachers, who Jains believe have revealed the truths of their faith.

SIDDHARTHA AND THE SWAN

There are many Buddhist and Jain myths that explore the theme of nonviolence and doing everything possible to reduce suffering. Several of the Buddhist tales have Siddhartha, the founder of Buddhism, as the main figure in the story.

When Siddhartha was a small boy, he used to sit in the palace gardens watching the birds and other animals. One day, a flock of white swans flew overhead. One of the swans suddenly dropped from the sky and landed at Siddhartha's feet. He could see an arrow sticking out of one of the swan's wings. Siddhartha pulled the swan toward him, wrapped it in his cloak, and vowed to look after the swan until it was better.

At that moment, his cousin Devadatta came running up to him, carrying a bow and arrow. He demanded that Siddhartha hand over the swan. Devadatta said that he had shot the swan, so it belonged to him. Siddhartha refused and the two boys began to argue. Neither of them would give in, so they agreed that the king should decide who kept the swan.

The king listened to both boys, but could not make up his mind. He asked his advisors, but they could not decide either. Finally, an old man appeared in front of them and said that it was not right to cause suffering. The king agreed, and the swan was given to Siddhartha.

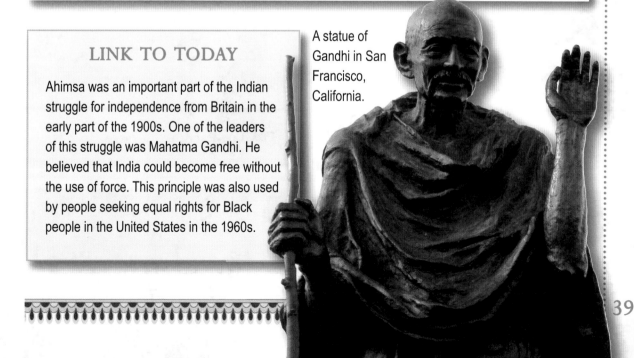

LINK TO TODAY

Ahimsa was an important part of the Indian struggle for independence from Britain in the early part of the 1900s. One of the leaders of this struggle was Mahatma Gandhi. He believed that India could become free without the use of force. This principle was also used by people seeking equal rights for Black people in the United States in the 1960s.

A statue of Gandhi in San Francisco, California.

INDIAN LEGACY

Many of the myths of Ancient India and the traditions of early Hinduism, Buddhism, and Jainism are very much alive today. They are seen in the everyday lives, festivals, buildings, art, and cultures of communities of these three faiths throughout the world, in countries such as the United States, Canada, and the United Kingdom.

As Hinduism grew in the Gupta Empire, great temples started to be built. The temple at Deogarh is one of the best known from this period. *Deogarh* means "fort of the gods." The temple is in modern-day Uttar Pradesh in India and is made of red sandstone. The outside walls are covered in carvings that tell the story of Vishnu. This style of architecture was used by temple builders for hundreds of years. An example is the Rajarajeswaram temple. Built around 1050 C.E., it is the largest temple in India. Many of these ancient temples are still in use today.

The last great temple to be built in India was the Hindu temple complex called Akshardham in New Delhi. It was officially opened in November 2005. Along with a vast temple, there are gardens, singing fountains, and an exhibition center. Today, there are more than 200 Hindu temples, 30 Jain temples, and many Buddhist meditation centers in the United States and Canada.

LINK TO TODAY

Many of the greatest modern Hindu temples have been built outside of India. The largest is the Shri Swaminarayan Mandir in London, completed in 1995. The first traditional Hindu temple in the United States was opened in Flushing, New York City, in 1977. The Malibu Hindu Temple in California is a large traditional Hindu temple completed in 1981.

MURUGAN AND THE YOKE

Many ancient temples in India have their own myths and stories associated with them. The Sri Nataraja temple in modern Tamil Nadu, southern India, is dedicated to Shiva. Palani is another of the six temples in Tamil Nadu and it is connected to the life of Murugan, the son of Shiva. This myth comes from the Sri Nataraja temple.

A wise man presented Shiva with two hills that were to be used as places of worship. Shiva accepted them and asked that the hills be transported to southern India. The wise man agreed. One day he met Idumban—a demon who had lost his demonic nature after losing a battle to Murugan. The wise man asked Idumban to collect the hills.

When Idumban arrived at the hills, a yoke (wooden frame) appeared from nowhere and eight snakes became ropes to tie the hills to the yoke. Idumban began the journey southward. Near Palani, he stopped to rest. When he tried to carry on, he found that he could not lift one of the hills. He climbed to the top of the hill and found a child playing. He tried to chase the child away.

The child refused to move. At that point, Idumban tried to grab the child to throw him off the hill. However, the child was Murugan in disguise and he killed Idumban on the spot. Murugan then brought Idumban back to life and made the demon his servant.

Below: The Shri Swaminarayan Mandir Hindu temple in Atlanta, Georgia, in the United States.

MYTHS IN FILM AND TV

The myths of Ancient India have been a source of ideas for modern Indian movie and TV program-makers. Many of the movies produced by Bollywood—the Hindi-language movie industry in Mumbai—are based on myths.

The first film that used Hindu myths was called *Markandaya*. It was made in 1935 and tells the story of a Hindu holy man. In 1958, an Indian film was released called *Bhookailas*. It told some of the stories of Ravana detailed in the *Ramayana*. A more recent movie is the cartoon *Hanuman* (2005), which tells the story of the god of the same name. Canadian movie director, James Cameron, admitted being influenced by Indian myths when he made the science fiction movie *Avatar* in 2009.

MYTH MOVIE SCRIPTS

Television companies have also used Indian myths for many dramas and these are very popular with viewers in India and with Hindus living in other parts of the world. The most popular was a series called *Ramayan*, which used the *Ramayana* as a source for its stories. It was broadcast every week for 78 weeks during 1987 and 1988 and it was watched by more than 100 million people. It remains the most popular program on Indian television. Between 1988 and 1990 *Mahabharat*, based on the *Mahabharata*, was broadcast over 75 weeks. It was also broadcast in Britain, Indonesia, and Fiji.

INDIAN MUSIC

In such a large and socially varied country as modern India, there are many different forms of music that are played. There are two types of classical music—Hindustani, which is mainly played in northern and central India; and Carnatic, which is played in the south of the country. It is believed that Carnatic music was given to the people of India by the goddess Saraswati.

Ancient folk and dance music is still played in India, especially during festivals such as Diwali and Navarati. The most popular form of music in India is called *filmi*. This is the style that is composed for the vast number of movies produced in the country.

One of the best-known Indian musicians and composers is Ravi Shankar.

Below: A dancer performs in *The Merchants of Bollywood*, a stage musical about the Indian movie industry.

Ravi started touring Europe and North America in the 1950s and he has done more than any other musician to bring Indian music to a wider audience. He has also worked with many classical and pop musicians over the years.

Indian music has influenced musicians all over the world. Raga Rock is Western rock and pop music that uses Indian styles and rhythms. It was in the 1960s that bands such as the Yardbirds, the Kinks and, most famously, The Beatles composed songs using Indian instruments. Hip-hop artists such as The Black Eyed Peas and Timbaland have used Indian music styles in their work.

Right: Transglobal Underground are musicians that use a fusion of Indian, African, and Western music styles. Here a player uses a sitar, an Indian stringed instrument.

Below: Indian traditional dancers perform at the Annual Dance Parade in Manhattan, New York City, in 2010.

INDIAN FOOD

The "nonkilling" tradition of many Indian people has excluded meat from their diets. For example, Hindus will not eat beef because the cow is a sacred animal. Most meals in modern-day India are based on such basic plant foods as millet, flour, rice, lentils, chickpeas, and kidney beans.

Food is an important part of many religious festivals. During Diwali, there are feasts for everybody taking part and children are given packets of candies. Food is an offering at temples and places of pilgrimage. One of the most spectacular is the Jain festival of Mahamastakabhisheka in which many foods, such as rice flour, milk, honey, and sugar, are poured over the head of a giant statue. Many of these customs relate to Ancient Indian myths.

Below: Indian food includes curries, rice, samosas, and naan bread.

TIME CHART

3300–1300 B.C.E.	Indus Valley Civilization
	Development of agriculture and industry
	Rise of first cities such as Harrapa, Lothal, and Kalibanga
1500–500 B.C.E.	Vedic civilization
1500–1100 B.C.E.	Idea of reincarnation developed and *Rig Veda* written
1000 B.C.E.	Mahajanapadas city-states emerge
900 B.C.E.	Kurukshetra War
600–527 B.C.E.	Life of Mahavira, the last of the Tirthankaras
500 B.C.E.	Mahajanapadas merged into 16 states
500 B.C.E.–**100** C.E.	*Ramayana* and the *Mahabarata* both compiled
circa 490–410 B.C.E.	Life of the Buddha
326 B.C.E.	Alexander the Great conquers part of northwest India
320–180 B.C.E.	Maurya Empire
320–298 B.C.E.	Reign of Chandragupta Maurya
300 B.C.E.	Jainism starts to spread
269–232 B.C.E.	Reign of Ashoka the Great
260 B.C.E.	Maurya Empire at greatest extent
260 B.C.E.	Ashoka the Great makes Buddhism the state religion
180 B.C.E.–**10** C.E.	Indo–Greek kingdoms in northern India
220 C.E.	Grand Anicut Dam built
240–280 C.E.	Reign of Sri Gupta, founder of Gupta Empire
300–550 C.E.	Gupta Empire
380–413 C.E.	Reign of Chandra Gupta II
1206–1526 C.E.	Delhi Sultanate
1526–1857 C.E.	Mughal Empire
1612 C.E.	British rule of India starts
1858–1947 C.E.	India directly ruled by Britain
1947 C.E.	India becomes independent
1869–1948 C.E.	Life of Mahatma Gandhi

[Some of the earlier dates in particular are approximate as accurate written records to not exist.]

GLOSSARY

Arabia The region of southwest Asia between the Red Sea and the Persian Gulf that includes such modern countries as Kuwait and Saudi Arabia

Brahma The god responsible for creating the Universe

Brahman Spirit that exists throughout all of the Universe

caste Position in society given at birth

city-state A small state dominated by one city

deities Gods and goddesses

devotees People who follow someone with passion

devotion Strong feelings for something

Diwali Hindu festival of light

enlightenment The state of being aware of, or awakened to, one's path in life and how to end suffering

epics Lengthy or grand poems

fortified Strengthened or protected

Ganesh The god of wisdom

golden age A period when art and science flourishes

immortality Able to live forever or to avoid death

karma The Hindu belief that what you do in this life will affect what you become in your next life

Lakshmi The goddess of wealth and prosperity

mobile Being able to move freely

outcasts People who are not a member of any caste

pilgrimage A journey to a place that has religious importance

pious Describing someone who is very religious

prophecy A prediction of what will happen in the future

purification Freeing someone of sin

reincarnation The continuous cycle of birth, life, death, and rebirth

sacrifice A human or an animal who is killed as an offering or gift to a god or goddess

scriptures Holy writings or religious texts

Shiva The god responsible for the destruction of the Universe

spirit An invisible force or power believed to exist within the natural world such as the soul of a dead person

subcontinent A large mass of land that is part of a major continent, for example India as part of Asia

textiles Fabrics made by weaving fibers

Vedas Sacred texts written in the Vedic period

virtuously Done for a good, worthwhile, or desirable reason

Vishnu The god responsible for preserving the Universe

LEARNING MORE

BOOKS

Ali, Daud. *Ancient India* (Passport to the Past). New York: Rosen Publishing, 2009.

Avari, Burjor. *India: The Ancient Past—A History of the Indian Sub-Continent from 7000 BC to AD 1200.* New York: Routledge, 2007.

Barr, Marilynn G. *India.* Dayton, OH: Teaching & Learning Co, 2003.

Holm, Kirsten. *Everyday Life in Ancient India.* New York: Rosen Publishing, 2012.

Hynson, Colin. *Discover Jainism.* London: Institute of Jainology, 2006.

Hynson, Colin. *Jain Tales.* London: Institute of Jainology, 2008.

Kenoyer, Jonathan Mark, and Kimberley Heuston. *The Ancient South Asian World.* New York: Oxford University Press, 2005.

Schomp, Virginia. *Ancient India* (People of the Ancient World). New York: Franklin Watts, 2005.

Husain, Shahrukh, and Bee Willey. *Indian Myths* (Stories from Ancient Civilisations). London: Evans Brothers, 2005.

WEBSITES

Asian Art Museum
www.asianart.org/

BBC History: Ancient India
www.bbc.co.uk/history/ancient/india/

British Museum: Ancient South Asia
www.britishmuseum.org/explore/cultures/asia/ancient_south_asia.aspx

Canadian Museum of Hindu Civilization
www.cmohc.com/

Hindu American Foundation
www.hafsite.org/

PBS—The Story of India
www.pbs.org/thestoryofindia/

INDEX